SUCCESS BLUEPRINT:

Easy Guide to Achieving Success

Alberto L. Wilson

TABLE OF CONTENT

CONCLUSIONS

- Reviewing your success blueprint and making adjustments
- Embracing a lifelong journey of growth and success.

60-DAYS SUCCESS CHALLENGE

VISION

PLANNING

ACTION

PERSISTENCE

LEARNING

ADAPTABILITY

CELEBRATION

LEGACY

INTRODUCTION

Are you tired of feeling like you're constantly spinning your wheels in life, going through the motions without making any real progress toward your dreams and goals? Do you find yourself looking at successful people and wondering what their secret is while feeling like you're missing out on some crucial piece of the puzzle? If so, this book is what you need to unlock your inner power and activate success.

"Success Blueprint: Easy Guide to Achieving Success" - the ultimate guide to unlocking your full potential and achieving the success you've always dreamed of. In this book, you'll discover the step-by-step blueprint for success that has been used by the world's most successful people, from entrepreneurs and athletes to artists and politicians.

Through powerful stories, actionable tips, and easy-to-follow exercises, you'll learn how to overcome the obstacles that have been holding you back, tap into your innate strengths, and create a life of purpose and fulfillment. Whether you're just starting on your journey or you're looking to take your success to the next level, this book is the ultimate guide to achieving your wildest dreams.

So if you're ready to stop settling for less than you deserve and start living the life you were meant to live, then grab your copy of "Success Blueprint: Easy Guide to Achieving Success" today and start building the life of your dreams!

"Success Blueprint: Easy Guide to Achieving Success" is a term used to describe a set of principles and strategies that can help individuals achieve their goals and reach their desired level of success. These principles and strategies are based on the experiences of successful people who have achieved their own goals and attained success in their respective fields.

The key components of a Success Blueprint include setting clear goals, creating a plan to achieve those goals, developing the necessary skills and knowledge to succeed, taking consistent action toward the goals, and remaining focused and committed throughout the process. Additionally, it's important to stay flexible and adaptable in the face of challenges and setbacks and to learn from failures and mistakes along the way.

The Success Blueprint also emphasizes the importance of personal growth and self-improvement, as well as building strong relationships and networks to support and motivate you along your journey. Other factors such as a positive mindset, perseverance, and a willingness to take calculated risks are also important components of the Success Blueprint.

Ultimately, the Success Blueprint is a roadmap that can help individuals define and achieve their definition of success. By following these principles and strategies, individuals can overcome obstacles, stay focused on their goals, and achieve the success they desire.

SUCCESS

↓

Hardwork

Persistence

Rejections

Late nights

Discipline

Failures

Risks

Chapter 1

WHY ARE SUCCESS BLUEPRINTS IMPORTANT?

A success blueprint is important because it provides a clear plan or roadmap for achieving success in a particular area or endeavor. Without a blueprint or plan, it can be difficult to know where to start, what steps to take, or what goals to work towards.

The mindset for success

A success mindset refers to a set of beliefs, attitudes, and habits that foster a positive and proactive approach to achieving one's goals and ambitions. Individuals with a success mindset tend to have a strong sense of self-efficacy, optimism, resilience, and perseverance, which help them overcome obstacles and setbacks along the way.

Once upon a time, there was a young man named Alex who dreamed of becoming a successful businessman. Alex had always been fascinated by the world of entrepreneurship, and he spent countless hours reading books, attending seminars, and watching videos to learn everything he could about starting and growing a business.

Despite his passion and drive, Alex faced many challenges along the way. He struggled to come up with a unique business idea and had trouble finding investors who believed in his vision. However, he refused to give up, and instead, he kept pushing forward, determined to turn his dream into a reality. Eventually, Alex came up with a brilliant business idea that he believed could change the world. He spent months refining his concept, building a team, and securing funding from investors who shared his vision. Finally, he launched his business, and to his amazement, it took off almost immediately.

Over the next few years, Alex's business grew rapidly, and he became one of the most successful entrepreneurs in his industry. He hired talented employees, expanded his product line, and opened new locations around the world. Along the way, he encountered many obstacles and setbacks, but he always found a way to overcome them and keep moving forward.

Looking back on his journey, Alex realized that his success was not just a result of his hard work and determination. It was also due to the support and encouragement he received from his friends, family, and mentors. He learned that no one achieves success alone and that it takes a team of dedicated and passionate individuals to bring a vision to life.

Today, Alex's business continues to thrive, and he is grateful for the opportunities and challenges that have shaped him into the successful entrepreneur he is today. He hopes to inspire others to pursue their dreams with the same passion and dedication that he did, knowing that anything is possible with hard work, perseverance, and a little bit of luck.

The mindset for success is a way of thinking that enables individuals to achieve their goals and reach their full potential. It involves cultivating a positive and growth-oriented mindset, focusing on personal development and learning, being resilient in the face of challenges, and taking proactive steps toward achieving one's goals.

The mindset for success involves adopting certain attitudes and habits that can help you achieve your goals and reach your full potential.

Some key characteristics of a success mindset include:

1. **Positive attitude**: Having a positive attitude can help you stay motivated and focused on your goals, even when faced with setbacks or challenges.

2. **Growth mindset:** A growth mindset means believing that your abilities can be developed through hard work and dedication. This mindset encourages learning, progress, and self-improvement.

3. **Persistence**: Success often requires perseverance and determination. A willingness to keep pushing forward in the face of obstacles is an essential part of a success mindset.

4. **Resilience**: Failure and setbacks are a natural part of any journey toward success. Resilience involves bouncing back from these challenges and using them as opportunities for growth.

5. **Goal-oriented**: Setting specific, measurable, achievable, relevant, and time-bound (SMART) goal is a crucial part of success. A success mindset involves being focused and driven toward achieving these goals.

6. **Continuous learning**: Successful people are often lifelong learners. They are open to new ideas, experiences, and perspectives, and they seek out opportunities for personal and professional growth.

7. **Self-discipline**: Success often requires self-discipline and the ability to prioritize tasks and manage time effectively. Developing good habits, such as setting and sticking to a routine, can help you stay focused and productive.

By adopting these attitudes and habits, you can cultivate a success mindset that will help you achieve your goals and realize your full potential.

Understanding Success

Success can be defined in many different ways, depending on an individual's goals, values, and priorities. Here are some common ways to understand success:

1. **Achieving a goal**: Success can be defined as achieving a specific goal or objective. This could be a personal goal, such as losing weight or learning a new skill, or a professional goal, such as meeting a sales target or launching a successful product.

2. **Fulfillment and happiness**: Success can also be defined as experiencing fulfillment and happiness in life. This may involve having meaningful relationships, engaging in activities that bring joy, and feeling a sense of purpose and contentment.

3. **Financial stability**: For some people, success may be defined as achieving financial stability or financial independence. This may involve earning a certain amount of money, having a comfortable lifestyle, or building wealth for the future.

4. **Making a difference**: Success can also be defined as making a positive impact on the world, whether through philanthropy, social activism, or creating a product or service that helps people.

5. **Personal growth and development**: Success can also be defined as continuous personal growth and development. This may involve learning new skills, overcoming challenges, and becoming a better version of oneself.

Ultimately, success is a subjective concept and can mean different things to different people. It is important to define success on your terms and align your goals and actions with what matters most to you.

Different types of success

There are different types of success, and what defines success can vary from person to person. Here are some common types of success:

1. **Professional success:** This type of success is often measured by career achievements, such as promotions, job satisfaction, and financial stability.

2. **Personal success:** This type of success is often measured by personal achievements, such as maintaining good health, strong relationships, and a sense of fulfillment and happiness.

3. **Academic success**: This type of success is often measured by educational achievements, such as obtaining degrees or certifications, and achieving academic goals.

4. **Financial success**: This type of success is often measured by financial achievements, such as accumulating wealth, having financial stability, and meeting financial goals.

5. **Creative success**: This type of success is often measured by creative achievements, such as creating artwork, writing a book, or composing music.

6. **Social success**: This type of success is often measured by social achievements, such as building strong relationships, having a supportive network, and making a positive impact in the community.

7. **Spiritual success**: This type of success is often measured by spiritual achievements, such as developing a sense of inner peace, connection to a higher power, and a strong sense of purpose.

It's important to note that success is not always measured by tangible achievements or external validation. It can also be measured by personal growth, overcoming challenges, and making a positive impact on the world. Ultimately, what defines success is subjective and depends on an individual's values, aspirations, and life experiences.

Characteristics of successful people

Successful people possess a range of characteristics that contribute to their achievements.

1. **Goal-oriented:** Successful people have clear goals and a strong sense of purpose. They set specific and measurable goals and develop plans to achieve them.

2. **Perseverance**: Successful people have the ability to persevere in the face of obstacles, setbacks, and failures. They don't give up easily and remain committed to their goals even when facing challenges.

3. **Positive attitude:** Successful people maintain a positive attitude and outlook. They approach challenges with optimism and view setbacks as opportunities to learn and grow.

4. **Self-discipline**: Successful people have the ability to prioritize and manage their time effectively. They maintain a strong work ethic and are committed to self-improvement.

5. **Adaptability**: Successful people are adaptable and flexible. They are able to adjust their strategies and plans in response to changing circumstances.

6. **Strong communication skills**: Successful people have strong communication skills. They are able to express their ideas clearly and persuasively, and they are able to listen actively and respond appropriately.

7. **Resilience:** Successful people have the ability to bounce back from adversity. They are able to recover from setbacks and continue moving forward.

8. **Focus:** Successful people have the ability to focus their energy and attention on the task at hand. They avoid distractions and are able to maintain their concentration.

9. **Creativity:** Successful people are often creative and innovative. They are able to generate new ideas and approaches to solving problems.

10. **Continuous learning:** Successful people are committed to continuous learning and self-improvement. They are open to feedback and seek out opportunities to develop new skills and knowledge.

Chapter 2

COMMON MISCONCEPTIONS ABOUT SUCCESS

Misconceptions about success are false beliefs or ideas that people have about what it takes to be successful.

There are many misconceptions about success that can hold people back from achieving their goals. Here are some common ones:

1. **Success is only for the lucky or the talented:** This is a common misconception that success is only for those who are born with talent or have had good luck. In reality, success comes from hard work, perseverance, and a willingness to learn and grow.

2. **Success means never failing:** Failure is a natural part of the journey to success. Many successful people have failed timelessly before achieving their goals. Success is about learning from failures and using them to move forward.

3. **Success is the same for everyone:** Success means different things to different people. It is important to define success on your terms and to

pursue goals that align with your values and passions.

4. **Success is permanent:** Success is not a permanent state. It requires ongoing effort and commitment to maintain, and success can be lost if one becomes complacent or stops striving for improvement.

5. **Success is all about money and fame:** Many people equate success with money and fame, but this is not necessarily true. Success can mean different things to different people. It could mean having a happy family life, pursuing a fulfilling career, or making a positive impact on society.

6. **Success is easy:** Another misconception is that success comes easy to those who are talented or lucky. In reality, success requires hard work, persistence, and a willingness to learn from failures and setbacks.

7. **Success is only for the young:** Some people believe that success is only achievable at a young age. However, success can be achieved at any age, and many people have achieved great things later in life.

8. **Success is a destination:** Success is often seen as a destination that one can reach and

then rest. However, success is a journey, and there are always new goals to achieve and challenges to overcome.

9. **Success is the result of individual effort:** While individual effort is important, success often requires the support and collaboration of others. Successful people often have mentors, allies, and a supportive network that helps them achieve their goals.

Overall, success is a complex and multifaceted concept that cannot be reduced to a single formula or definition. It is important to recognize that success can mean different things to different people and that it is achieved through a combination of hard work, perseverance, and support from others.

Developing a Success Mindset

Developing a success mindset is the process of adopting a positive and growth-oriented attitude towards life and work that enables you to achieve your goals and overcome challenges. It involves cultivating a strong belief in your abilities, focusing on solutions instead of problems, embracing failures as opportunities for learning and growth, and maintaining a persistent and resilient mindset.

A success mindset requires a commitment to personal and professional development, a willingness to take risks, and a willingness to learn from mistakes. It also involves setting clear goals and taking consistent actions toward achieving them.

In essence, developing a success mindset involves shifting your mindset from one that is fixed and limiting to one that is open and empowering, which allows you to approach life with confidence, optimism, and a willingness to take on new challenges.

Believing in yourself

Believing in oneself means having confidence and trust in one's abilities, judgments, and decisions. It involves developing a positive self-image and a strong sense of self-worth. When you believe in yourself, you are more likely to take risks, pursue your goals, and handle setbacks and failures. Believing in oneself is a crucial aspect of personal development and can lead to greater success and happiness in life.

1. **Focus on your strengths**: Everyone has unique strengths and talents. Focus on what you're good at and use those strengths to your advantage.

2. **Challenge negative self-talk:** Pay attention to the negative thoughts that may be holding you back. Challenge them with positive affirmations and remind yourself of your accomplishments.

3. **Set achievable goals:** Setting small, achievable goals can help build your confidence and belief

in yourself. Celebrate your successes, no matter how small they may seem.

4. **Practice self-care:** Taking care of yourself physically and mentally can help boost your confidence and belief in yourself. Make sure to get enough sleep, exercise regularly, eat a healthy diet, and take time to relax and recharge.

5. **Surround yourself with positive people:** Surrounding yourself with people who believe in you and support you can help reinforce your own belief in yourself.

Believing in yourself is a process that takes time and effort. Be patient and focus on progress rather than perfection.

Chapter 3

CULTIVATING A POSITIVE ATTITUDE

Cultivating a positive attitude involves intentionally adopting a mindset that focuses on the positive aspects of life, rather than dwelling on negative thoughts and experiences.

Having a positive attitude can have a significant impact on your life, improving your relationships, work, and overall well-being. Here are some tips on cultivating a positive attitude:

- **Focus on gratitude**: Take time to appreciate the good things in your life, and focus on what you have rather than what you don't have. Write out a list of things you're grateful for each day.

- **Practice mindfulness:** Mindfulness is an exercise of being present in the moment, without judgment. When you are mindful, you can easily let go of negative thoughts and emotions.

- **Surround yourself with positivity:** Spend time with people who have a positive attitude, and avoid negative influences. Listen to uplifting music or read inspirational books.

- **Use positive affirmation**: Replace negative self-talk with positive affirmations. Instead of declaring "I can't do this," say "I am capable and confident."

- **Take care of your body**: Exercise regularly, eat a healthy diet, and get enough sleep. Taking care of your physical health can have a significant impact on your mental and emotional well-being.

- **Focus on solutions, not problems:** When faced with a challenge, focus on finding a solution rather than dwelling on the problem. Look for opportunities to learn and grow.

Overcoming fear of failure

The fear of failure is a common obstacle that can hold you back from pursuing your goals and achieving success. Here are some tips on overcoming the fear of failure:

1. **Change your perspective:** Instead of seeing failure as a negative outcome, view it as an opportunity to learn and grow. Failure is a natural part of the learning process, and every successful person has failed at some point.

2. **Take action:** Sometimes, the fear of failure can prevent you from taking action. Start with small

steps, and gradually work your way up to bigger challenges. Each step you take will build your confidence and reduce your fear.

3. **Visualize success:** Visualization is a powerful tool for overcoming fear. Imagine yourself succeeding in your goal, and focus on the positive outcomes of your success.

4. **Embrace failure:** Instead of avoiding failure, embrace it. When you fail, take the time to reflect on what you've learned and use it to improve your future efforts.

5. **Seek support:** Surround yourself with supportive people who believe in you and your goals. They can encourage and help you overcome your fear of failure.

6. **Practice self-compassion:** Be kind and gentle with yourself. Remember that everyone experiences failure and setbacks, and it doesn't define your worth or abilities.

Overcoming the fear of failure is a process that takes time and effort. Be patient and celebrate your triumphs along the way.

Embracing challenges

Embracing challenges refers to adopting a positive and proactive mindset when facing difficulties or obstacles. It involves recognizing that challenges are opportunities for growth, learning, and self-improvement, rather than seeing them as threats or sources of stress.

Embracing challenges can be a great way to grow and develop as a person, as well as to achieve your goals. Here are some tips on how to embrace challenges:

1. **Change your mindset**: Instead of seeing challenges as obstacles, try to see them as opportunities to learn and grow. This change in mindset can make all the difference.

2. **Break the challenge down into smaller tasks:** When faced with a daunting challenge, it can be helpful to break it down into smaller, more manageable tasks. This can help you to stay focused and motivated.

3. **Get outside your comfort zone:** It's important to challenge yourself and try new things in order to grow. This can be uneasy, but it's crucial for personal growth.

4. **Accept failure as part of the process:** Failure is inevitable when taking on challenges. Instead of being discouraged, see it as an opportunity to learn and grow.

5. **Seek support:** Don't be afraid to ask for help or seek support from others. This can be a great way to gain new perspectives and ideas.

6. **Celebrate your successes:** When you overcome a challenge, take the time to celebrate your success. This can be a great way to boost your confidence and motivation for future challenges.

Chapter 4

SELF-DISCOVERY

Self-discovery is the process of gaining insight into one's personality, values, beliefs, strengths, weaknesses, and life goals. It involves a journey of self-exploration, introspection, and reflection to better understand oneself and uncover the hidden aspects of one's personality. This process can involve a range of activities such as journaling, meditation, therapy, personal development courses, traveling, or any other activity that helps an individual gain a deeper understanding of themselves.

Through self-discovery, individuals can cultivate a better sense of self-awareness, self-acceptance, and self-love, which can lead to greater personal growth and fulfillment in life.

Defining success for yourself

Defining success for yourself involves determining what goals and achievements are important to you personally, rather than simply following society's or others' expectations. To define success for yourself, it is helpful to reflect on your values, passions, and long-term aspirations. What do you truly care about? What brings you joy and fulfillment? What kind of life do you want to lead in the future?

Once you have a clear understanding of your values and aspirations, you can begin to set goals and metrics for success that align with these priorities. For example, success might mean achieving a certain level of financial security, building strong relationships with loved ones, pursuing a meaningful career, making a positive impact in your community, or simply finding happiness and contentment in daily life.

It's important to remember that success is subjective and can look different for everyone. What matters most is that you are pursuing goals and achievements that are authentic to you and bring you a sense of purpose and fulfillment.

Defining success for yourself is a highly personal and subjective process. Here are some steps you can take to define success for yourself:

1. **Reflect on your values and goals:** Think about what is most important to you in life and what you want to achieve in the short-term and long term.

2. **Consider different areas of your life:** Success can be defined in various areas of life, such as career, relationships, health, personal development, etc. Consider which areas are most important to you and how you would like to achieve success in those areas.

3. **Determine your metrics of success:** Rather than relying on external measures of success

such as money or fame, identify your criteria for success. For example, you might define success in your career as achieving a work-life balance, making a positive impact on others, or constantly learning and growing.

4. **Set specific goals:** Once you have a sense of what success means to you, set specific goals that align with your values and criteria for success. Make sure these goals are challenging yet attainable.

Identifying your strengths and weaknesses

There are several ways to identify your strengths and weaknesses:

1. **Self-reflection:** Spend some time alone and think about your past experiences, achievements, and challenges. Ask yourself what you did well and where you struggled. Write down your thoughts to help you organize them.

2. **Feedback from others:** Ask friends, family, colleagues, or mentors for feedback on your strengths and weaknesses. They may be able to foster insights that you haven't considered.

3. **Personality tests:** Consider taking a personality test, such as the Myers-Briggs Type Indicator or

the Big Five Personality Traits. These tests can help you identify your strengths and weaknesses based on your personality traits.

4. **Skill assessments:** Take a skill assessment test to identify your strengths and weaknesses in specific areas, such as communication, problem-solving, or teamwork.

5. **Performance reviews:** Review past performance evaluations or feedback from managers to identify areas where you excel and areas where you need improvement.

Remember that identifying your strengths and weaknesses is just the first step. The next step is to create a plan to develop your strengths and work on your weaknesses. By doing so, you can evolve into a well-rounded and effective person.

Setting goals that align with your values and purpose

Setting goals that align with your values and purpose involves identifying what is most important to you and creating objectives that reflect those priorities.

Values are the principles and beliefs that guide your decision-making and help you determine what is meaningful and important in your life. Your purpose is your reason for being, your unique mission, and the overarching goal you are striving to achieve. When you set goals that align with your values and purpose, you are more likely to feel motivated, fulfilled, and satisfied with your progress and accomplishments.

For example, if one of your core values is health and fitness, and your purpose is to live a long, active, and healthy life, you might set a goal to run a marathon or complete a triathlon. This goal aligns with your values of health and fitness and supports your purpose of living a long and active life. To set goals that align with your values and purpose, start by identifying your core values and reflecting on your purpose or mission. Then, create goals that support those values and purpose. As you work towards your goals, continue to evaluate whether they are still aligned with your values and purpose, and adjust them as needed.

Setting goals that align with your values and purpose is a crucial aspect of achieving success and fulfillment in life. Here are some steps that can help you in setting such goals:

1. **Identify your values:** The first step in setting goals that align with your values is to identify what is most important to you. Consider the values that guide your decisions, beliefs, and actions.

2. **Determine your purpose:** Ask yourself what motivates and inspires you. What do you want to achieve in life? Your purpose should reflect your passions, talents, and interests.

3. **Set specific and measurable goals:** Once you have identified your values and purpose, it's time to set specific and measurable goals that align with them. Your goals should be realistic and achievable within a specific timeframe.

4. **Create an action plan:** To achieve your goals, you need to create an action plan. Break down your goals into smaller, manageable tasks, and assign deadlines to each of them.

5. **Stay focused and motivated:** Finally, it's essential to stay focused and motivated throughout the process. Keep your goals in mind and remind yourself of your values and purpose regularly. Celebrate your successes and learn from your failures.

Setting goals that align with your values and purpose is a continuous process. It requires self-reflection, evaluation, and adjustment. However, the rewards of achieving such goals are immeasurable, both personally and professionally.

Chapter 5

PLANNING FOR SUCCESS

Success
^
Ideas
^
Plan
^
Execute

Planning for success involves creating a roadmap or strategy that outlines the steps needed to achieve your desired outcome or goal. It involves setting specific, measurable, and achievable objectives and determining the resources, skills, and support you will need to reach them.

Creating a roadmap for achieving your goals

The roadmap for achieving your goals is a step-by-step plan that outlines the actions you need to take to reach your desired outcome. It involves breaking down your goals into smaller, manageable tasks and creating a timeline for completing each task. Here are some steps to follow.

1. **Identify your goals**: Begin by identifying the specific goals you want to achieve, ensuring that they are aligned with your values and purpose.

2. **Break down your goals into smaller tasks:** Break down your goals into smaller, more manageable tasks or milestones, each with a clear timeline and deadline.

3. **Prioritize your tasks:** Prioritize your tasks based on their level of importance and urgency, and create a schedule or timeline for completing them.

4. **Determine the resources needed:** Determine the resources you will need to accomplish your tasks, such as time, money, materials, and support from others.

5. **Develop a plan of action:** Create a detailed plan of action that outlines the specific steps you

need to take to achieve your goals, including timelines, deadlines, and checkpoints for monitoring progress.

6. **Stay focused and motivated:** Stay focused and motivated by reviewing your progress regularly, celebrating your achievements, and making adjustments to your plan as needed.

7. **Evaluate your progress:** Evaluate your progress regularly to determine whether you are on track to achieving your goals, and make adjustments to your plan as needed.

Creating a roadmap for achieving your goals is a critical step toward success. By breaking down your goals into smaller, achievable tasks and creating a clear plan of action, you can stay organized, focused, and motivated to achieve your objectives.

Breaking down your goals into actionable steps

Breaking down your goals into actionable steps is an important part of achieving success. By breaking down your goals into smaller, manageable tasks, you can create a roadmap for achieving your desired outcome and stay motivated throughout the process. steps you can take to break down your goals into actionable steps:

1. **Identify your goal:** Start by clearly defining your goal and what you want to achieve.

2. **Brainstorm:** Write down all the tasks that you think are necessary to achieve your goal. This can be a brainstorming session, where you list all the things that come to your mind.

3. **Organize and categorize:** Organize the tasks into categories or themes that make sense to you. For example, you can group all the tasks related to research, planning, execution, and evaluation.

4. **Prioritize:** Prioritize the tasks in order of importance and urgency. This will help you to focus on the most critical tasks and avoid getting bogged down by less important ones.

5. **Break it down:** Break down each task into smaller, more manageable steps. Each step should be specific, measurable, and achievable. For example, if your goal is to write a book, one task might be to research your topic. You could break that task down into smaller steps such as finding sources, taking notes, and organizing your findings.

6. **Assign a deadline:** Assign a deadline to each step to help you stay on track and monitor progress.

7. **Take action:** Start taking action on the tasks and steps that you have identified. Remember to regularly monitor progress, adjust your plan as needed, and celebrate your achievements along the way.

By breaking down your goals into actionable steps, you can avoid feeling overwhelmed and create a clear path toward achieving your desired outcome.

Developing a daily routine for success

Developing a daily routine for success is a great way to stay focused, motivated, and productive. Here are some steps you can take to develop a daily routine for success:

1. **Set goals:** Start by setting daily goals that align with your larger, long-term goals. Your goals should be specific, measurable, and achievable.

2. **Prioritize your tasks:** Prioritize your tasks for the day based on their level of importance and urgency. Focus on the most critical tasks first.

3. **Create a schedule:** Create a schedule that allows you to allocate time for each task. Be realistic about how much time each task will take

and make sure you allow for breaks and downtime.

4. **Create a morning routine:** Start your day with a morning routine that prepares you for success. This could include exercise, meditation, or reading a book.

5. **Stay organized:** Keep your workspace and schedule organized to help you stay focused and avoid distractions.

6. **Minimize distractions:** Minimize distractions by turning off notifications and setting aside specific times to check email or social media.

7. **Take breaks:** Take regular breaks to recharge and avoid burnout. This could include taking a walk outside or doing a quick stretch.

8. **Review your progress:** At the end of each day, review your progress towards your goals and identify areas where you can improve. Celebrate your achievements and make adjustments as needed.

Remember, developing a daily routine takes time and effort, and it's important to be flexible and adaptable as your needs and circumstances change.

Examples of daily routine

Example 1:

6:00 AM - Wake up and get out of bed

6:15 AM - Brush teeth and wash face

6:30 AM - Exercise or go for a morning walk

7:00 AM - Shower and get dressed

7:30 AM - Have breakfast

8:00 AM - Commute to work or start working from home

12:00 PM - Take a lunch break

1:00 PM - Continue working

6:00 PM - Finish work and commute back home

7:00 PM - Have dinner

8:00 PM - Relax or engage in a hobby

10:00 PM - Get ready for bed

10:30 PM - Go to sleep

Example 2:

7:00 AM - Wake up and get out of bed

7:15 AM - Brush teeth and wash face

7:30 AM - Prepare breakfast and eat

8:00 AM - Commute to school or start studying

12:00 PM - Take a lunch break

1:00 PM - Continue studying or attending classes

5:00 PM - Finish studying or attending classes

6:00 PM - Have dinner

7:00 PM - Exercise or engage in a hobby

8:00 PM - Relax or socialize with friends

10:00 PM - Get ready for bed

10:30 PM - Go to sleep

Example 3:

6:00 AM - Wake up and get out of bed
6:15 AM - Meditate or practice yoga
7:00 AM - Shower and get dressed
7:30 AM - Have breakfast
8:00 AM - Start work from home or commute to work
12:00 PM - Take a lunch break
1:00 PM - Continue working
6:00 PM - Finish work and commute back home
7:00 PM - Have dinner
8:00 PM - Watch TV or read a book
9:00 PM - Prepare for the next day
10:00 PM - Get ready for bed
10:30 PM - Go to sleep

Chapter 6

SETTING GOALS FOR SUCCESS

Setting goals for success involves identifying specific objectives that you want to achieve and creating a plan to work toward them. The importance of goal success is that it can help you to stay motivated, focused, and accountable. When you have a clear vision of what you want to accomplish, it becomes easier to prioritize your time and resources and track your progress.

Here are some reasons why setting goals for success is important:

1. **Provides direction:** Goals provide a sense of direction and purpose, helping you to focus your efforts toward achieving a specific outcome.

2. **Increases motivation:** Having a clear goal in mind can increase your motivation to work towards it, especially if the goal is meaningful and aligned with your values.

3. **Boosts confidence:** When you set goals and achieve them, it can increase your confidence and self-esteem, giving you a sense of accomplishment and satisfaction.

4. **Enhances decision-making:** Goals can help you to make better decisions by providing a framework for evaluating options and choosing the best course of action.

5. **Improves productivity:** When you have clear goals, it becomes easier to prioritize tasks and focus on what matters most, leading to increased productivity and efficiency.

In summary, setting goals for success is important because it provides direction, increases motivation and confidence, enhances decision-making, and improves productivity. By setting goals and working towards them, you can achieve greater success and fulfillment in your personal and professional life.

Types of goals

There are many types of goals, but here are some common categories:

- **Personal Goals:** These are goals that focus on individual improvements, such as learning a new skill, improving health and fitness, or developing better habits

- **Career Goals:** These are goals related to one's profession, such as getting a promotion, earning a certain amount of money, or starting a business.

- **Academic Goals:** These are goals related to education, such as completing a degree, getting good grades, or learning a new language.

- **Relationship Goals:** These are goals related to interpersonal relationships, such as building better friendships, finding a partner, or improving communication with family members.

- **Financial Goals:** These are goals related to money, such as saving for retirement, paying off debt, or buying a house.

- **Spiritual Goals:** These are goals related to one's beliefs and values, such as practicing meditation, volunteering, or attending religious services.

- **Creative Goals:** These are goals related to artistic expression, such as writing a novel, painting a masterpiece, or composing music.

- **Travel Goals**: These are goals related to travel and exploration, such as visiting a new country, going on a road trip, or taking a cruise.

These are just a few examples, and there are many more types of goals depending on the individual's interests, values, and priorities.

SMART goal-setting

SMART goal-setting is a popular strategy for setting and achieving goals. The acronym SMART stands for Specific, Measurable, Achievable, Relevant, and Time-bound. Here's how to set a SMART goal:

1. **Specific:** Clearly define what you want to achieve. Be as specific as possible, including details like what, where, and how. For instance, instead of setting a goal to "get fit," you might set a goal to "lose 10 pounds by going to the gym 3 times per week and cutting out junk food."

2. **Measurable:** Make sure your goal can be measured in some way. This will help you track your progress and know when you've achieved it. Using the example above, losing 10 pounds is a measurable goal.

3. **Achievable**: Make sure your goal is realistic and achievable. It should challenge you, but also be something that you can realistically accomplish. Going from no exercise to going to the gym 7 days a week is not an achievable goal for most people.

4. **Relevant:** Make sure your goal is relevant to your overall objectives and priorities. It should be something that matters to you and that you're passionate about. For example, if your overall

objective is to improve your health, then getting in shape would be a relevant goal.

5. **Time-bound:** Set a deadline for when you want to achieve your goal. This will help you stay focused and motivated. Using the example above, you might set a deadline of 3 months to lose 10 pounds.

By setting a SMART goal, you'll have a clear roadmap for achieving what you want. It will help you stay focused, and motivated, and track your progress along the way.

Examples of smart goals

A SMART goal is a goal that is Specific, Measurable, Achievable, Relevant, and Time-bound.

- Specific: I want to lose weight.
- Measurable: I want to lose 10 pounds in the next 2 months by exercising 3 times a week and eating a healthy, balanced diet.
- Achievable: Losing 10 pounds in 2 months is achievable and realistic, and exercising 3 times a week and eating a healthy diet is manageable.
- Relevant: Losing weight is relevant to my health and well-being.
- Time-bound: I want to achieve this goal in the next 2 months.

- Specific: I want to improve my writing skills.
- Measurable: I want to write 500 words a day for the next 30 days and submit at least one article for publication.
- Achievable: Writing 500 words a day is achievable, and submitting at least one article for publication is realistic.
- Relevant: Improving my writing skills will help me in my career and personal life.
- Time-bound: I want to achieve this goal in the next 30 days.

- Specific: I want to increase my sales.
- Measurable: I want to increase my sales by 20% in the next quarter by expanding my customer base and introducing a new product.
- Achievable: Increasing sales by 20% is achievable, and expanding my customer base and introducing a new product are realistic strategies.
- Relevant: Increasing sales is relevant to my business success.
- Time-bound: I want to achieve this goal in the next quarter.

Creating an action plan

Creating an action plan is the next step after setting a SMART goal. An action plan is a detailed plan that outlines the specific steps you need to take to achieve your goal. Here's how to create an action plan:

1. **Break down your goal into smaller, achievable tasks**: Identify the specific actions that need to be taken to achieve your goal. Write down each task in a list or a spreadsheet.

2. **Set deadlines for each task:** Determine when each task needs to be completed to achieve your overall goal within your desired timeframe. Be realistic with your deadlines, but also challenge yourself to stay on track.

3. **Assign responsibility:** Determine who will be responsible for completing each task. This could be you or someone else who is helping you achieve your goal.

4. **Identify resources:** Determine what resources you need to complete each task. This could include tools, materials, or support from others.

5. **Monitor progress:** Regularly monitor your progress to ensure that you are on track to achieving your goal. This will help you stay motivated and adjust your action plan if necessary.

6. **Celebrate milestones:** Celebrate your successes along the way to keep yourself motivated and maintain your momentum.

Example of an action plan

An action plan is a living document that can be adjusted as you go. If you encounter obstacles or things don't go according to plan, adjust your action plan accordingly and keep moving forward.

GOAL: Improve physical fitness and lose 10 pounds in the next 3 months.

1. Step 1:Set a specific and measurable goal

2. Step 2: Determine the necessary actions.
- Join a gym and attend at least 3 times per week.
- Incorporate more fruits and vegetables into meals.
- Reduce processed food and sugar intake.
- Drink at least 8 glasses of water daily.
- Track progress by weighing myself every week.

3. Step 3: Create a timeline and prioritize actions
- Week 1: Join the gym and schedule workouts, start tracking water intake.
- Week 2-3: Focus on reducing processed food and sugar intake, and increasing vegetable consumption.
- Week 4-6: Increase cardio workouts and weight lifting, and track food intake.
- Week 7-9: Incorporate more protein and fiber into meals, monitor progress weekly.

- Week 10-12: Maintain healthy habits and continue tracking progress.

4. Step 4: Identify potential barriers and create solutions.
- **Barrier:** Lack of motivation to go to the gym.
- **Solution:** Find an accountability partner or hire a personal trainer.

- **Barrier:** Temptation to eat unhealthy snacks.
- **Solution:** Keep healthy snacks readily available and limit temptation by removing unhealthy snacks from the house.

5. Step 5: Monitor and evaluate progress
- Weigh myself weekly and track food and exercise in a journal or app.
- Assess progress and adjust action plan as necessary.

By following this action plan, one can achieve their goal of improving their physical fitness and losing 10 pounds in the next 3 months.

SUCCESS

SMART-Goals

Specific

Measurable

Achievable

Relevant

Time-bound

Action plan

Chapter 7

TAKING ACTION

Taking action on success means putting in the effort and taking the necessary steps to build upon the success that has been achieved. Success is not just about reaching a specific goal or milestone but also about maintaining that success and striving for even greater achievements. Taking action on success involves developing a plan, setting new goals, and taking proactive steps to continue to grow and improve. It also means staying focused and committed to the process, even when faced with challenges or setbacks.

By taking action on success, individuals can continue to build upon their achievements and reach new levels of success in their personal and professional lives.

Overcoming procrastination and taking consistent action

Procrastination is a typical problem that most people struggle with. It's easy to get distracted, lose motivation, or feel overwhelmed when faced with a task that requires effort or discipline. There are several strategies you can use to overcome procrastination and take consistent action toward your goals.

1. **Set clear goals:** It's important to have a clear understanding of what you want to achieve and why it's important to you. Write out your goals, and break them down into smaller and achievable steps.

2. **Create a plan:** Once you have your goals and steps in place, create a plan for how you will accomplish them. Use a planner, calendar, or app to schedule time for each task, and stick to your schedule as much as possible.

3. **Identify your distractions:** Be aware of the things that distract you from your work, whether it's social media, email, or other activities. Limit your exposure to these distractions by turning off notifications, blocking websites, or using apps that help you stay focused.

4. **Practice self-discipline:** Self-discipline is the ability to control your actions and emotions, even when you don't feel like doing something. Develop habits that support your goals, such as waking up early, exercising regularly, and taking breaks when you need them.

5. **Focus on progress, not perfection:** Remember that progress is more important than perfection. Don't get discouraged if you make mistakes or don't achieve your goals right away.

Celebrate your successes, and use your failures as opportunities to learn and grow.

6. **Reward yourself:** Give yourself rewards for completing tasks or achieving milestones. This can be as simple as taking a break, treating yourself to something you enjoy, or sharing your success with others.

By using these strategies, you can overcome procrastination and take consistent action toward your goals.

Dealing with failure and setbacks

Failure and setbacks are situations in which one's efforts, plans, or expectations do not produce the desired outcome or result. Failure refers to a complete lack of success or a significant inability to achieve one's goals, while setbacks typically involve temporary or partial obstacles that hinder progress toward a goal.

Both failure and setbacks are a common part of life and can occur in any aspect of life, whether personal, professional, or academic. They can arise due to a range of factors, including external circumstances beyond one's control, poor planning or execution, or unforeseen obstacles.

While experiencing failure or setbacks can be discouraging, they can also provide valuable learning opportunities and serve as a catalyst for growth and improvement. It is important to embrace these experiences as an opportunity to learn from mistakes, reassess goals, and develop resilience and perseverance.

Dealing with failure and setbacks can be a challenging and difficult experience, but it's important to remember that setbacks are a natural part of the learning process, and everyone experiences failure at some point in their lives. Here are some strategies that can help you overcome setbacks and learn from your failures:

1. **Accept your feelings:** It's normal to feel disappointed, frustrated, or sad after a setback. Allow yourself to feel these emotions and acknowledge them without judgment. This can help you process your emotions and move along.

2. **Analyze what went wrong:** Take the time to reflect on what caused the setback and analyze what went wrong. This can help you identify areas where you can improve, and make changes to your approach in the future.

3. **Learn from your mistakes:** Use your setback as an opportunity to learn, discover and grow. Think about what you can do differently next time to avoid making the same mistakes.

4. **Reframe your mindset:** Reframe your mindset from a negative one to a positive one. Instead of seeing the setback as a failure, see it as a

learning opportunity that will help you grow and develop.

5. **Seek support:** Reach out to family, friends, or a mentor for support. Talking about your setbacks and failures can help you process your emotions and gain a new perspective.

6. **Keep going:** Remember that setbacks are temporary, and success is often the result of persistence and resilience. Keep pushing forward, and don't let setbacks discourage you from pursuing your goals.

Setbacks and failures are a natural part of the learning process, and it's important to approach them with a growth mindset. Use setbacks as an opportunity to learn and grow, and seek support from others when you need it. Remember to stay persistent and keep moving forward, even in the face of challenges.

Developing resilience and perseverance

Resilience is the ability to adapt and recover in the face of adversity, challenges, or difficult circumstances. It involves having the strength and flexibility to withstand and overcome difficult situations, and the ability to bounce back from setbacks or failures. Resilience is not just about being tough, but also about being able to manage emotions, cope with stress, and maintain a positive outlook in the face of adversity.

Perseverance, on the other hand, is the ability to persist in pursuing a goal despite obstacles or difficulties. It involves having the determination and motivation to continue working towards a desired outcome, even when faced with setbacks or challenges. Perseverance often requires a combination of mental and emotional strength, as well as discipline, focus, and a willingness to learn from failures and mistakes. Both resilience and perseverance are important qualities that can help individuals overcome challenges and achieve success in their personal and professional lives.

Developing these qualities takes practice, self-awareness, and a willingness to learn and grow from adversity. Here are some tips that may help:

1. **Practice self-care:** Take care of your physical and emotional needs by getting enough sleep, eating a healthy diet, exercising regularly, and engaging in activities that bring you joy and relaxation.

2. **Develop a growth mindset:** Focus on the process of learning and growing rather than just the result. Take up challenges and view losses as opportunities for growth.

3. **Cultivate a support network:** Surround yourself with positive, supportive people who can provide encouragement and help you stay motivated.

4. **Learn from setbacks:** When faced with setbacks or failures, reflect on what you can learn from the experience and how you can use that knowledge to improve in the future.

5. **Practice mindfulness:** Develop the ability to stay present and focused on the present moment, rather than getting bogged down by worries about the future or regrets about the past.

Building resilience and perseverance is not a one-time event but a process that requires ongoing effort and commitment. With patience and persistence, you can develop the skills you need to bounce back from challenges and achieve your goals.

Chapter 8

BUILDING A SUPPORT SYSTEM

Building a support system refers to developing a network of people who can provide emotional, practical, and/or informational support during challenging times. A support system may include family members, friends, colleagues, mentors, or professionals such as therapists or counselors. Having a support system can be crucial for improving mental health and well-being, managing stress and anxiety, and coping with life's challenges.

1. **Identify people who can offer support:** This may include people you already know or individuals you meet through support groups, clubs, or social activities.

2. **Communicate your needs:** Let people know what kind of support you need, whether it's a listening ear, practical help, or advice.

3. **Be a good listener:** Building a support system is a two-way street. Make sure you are available to offer support to others in your network when they need it.

4. **Seek professional help when necessary:** A mental health professional can be an important

part of your support system. Consider seeking counseling or therapy if you are struggling with mental health issues or need additional support.

Building a support system takes time and effort, and it's important to nurture these relationships over time. It's also important to be realistic about what your support system can offer, and not rely solely on others for your well-being.

Surrounding yourself with positive influences

Surrounding yourself with positive influences can have a great impact on your mental and emotional well-being. Here are some ways to create a positive environment:

1. **Surround yourself with supportive people:** Spend time with people who encourage and uplift you, and avoid those who bring you down or make you feel bad about yourself.

2. **Focus on positivity:** Try to maintain a positive attitude and outlook, and look for the good in every situation. This can enable you to stay inspired and resilient in the face of challenges.

3. **Practice gratitude:** Take time to appreciate the good things in your life and express gratitude for

them. This can help divert your focus away from negative beliefs and emotions.

4. **Engage in activities that bring you joy:** Spend time doing things that make you happy and bring you a sense of fulfillment. This can help boost your mood and overall well-being.

5. **Seek out positive media and entertainment:** Watch uplifting movies, read inspiring books, or listen to uplifting music that puts you in a positive frame of mind.

Creating a positive environment takes effort and time, but the benefits can be significant. By surrounding yourself with positivity, you can improve your mental and emotional health, boost your self-esteem, and improve your overall quality of life.

Networking and building relationships

Networking is the process of creating and maintaining professional relationships with other individuals or groups in order to achieve personal or professional goals. It involves meeting new people, building rapport, and exchanging information and ideas.

Building relationships is the process of establishing and maintaining emotional connections with others over time. This can involve both personal and professional relationships, and it often requires ongoing communication, trust, and mutual respect.

In the context of business, networking and building relationships can be important for a variety of reasons, including expanding your professional network, finding new job opportunities, developing new partnerships or collaborations, and increasing your influence and visibility within your industry or community.

Networking and building relationships are important skills that can benefit you both personally and professionally. Here are some tips on how to effectively network and build relationships:

1. **Attend events:** Attend networking events, conferences, and industry gatherings where you can meet new people and make connections.

2. **Be prepared:** Before attending an event, research the attendees and make a list of the people you want to meet. Prepare a short elevator pitch about yourself that highlights your skills and accomplishments.

3. **Listen:** When meeting someone new, listen carefully to what they have to say. This shows that you are interested in them and enables you to build a connection.

4. **Follow-up:** After meeting someone, send a follow-up email or message to thank them for

their time and to express your interest in staying in touch.

5. **Be genuine:** Don't just network for the sake of networking. Build relationships with people because you genuinely value their skills, insights, and perspectives.

6. **Offer value:** Share your expertise, offer to help others with their projects, and provide value in any way you can. This builds trust and strengthens relationships.

7. **Maintain relationships:** Stay in touch with people, whether it's through social media, email, or in-person meetings. Remember to celebrate their achievements and offer support during challenging times.

By following these tips, you can effectively network and build strong relationships that can benefit you both personally and professionally.

Seeking mentorship and guidance

Seeking mentorship and guidance refers to the act of looking for someone who has more experience, knowledge, and skills than oneself to offer advice, support, and direction in a particular area or field. The mentor or guide is typically someone who has already achieved success in the area of interest and can offer valuable insights and advice to help the mentee or seeker develop their skills and knowledge.

Mentorship and guidance can take many forms, including one-on-one meetings, group sessions, online forums, and structured mentorship programs. It is a valuable tool for personal and professional growth, as it provides the mentee with the opportunity to learn from someone who has already achieved success and can offer guidance and support throughout their journey.

Seeking mentorship and guidance can help individuals to develop new skills, gain valuable insights, build confidence, and achieve their goals more effectively.

There are several ways you can seek mentorship and guidance:

1. **Identify your needs:** Start by identifying what specific areas you need mentorship and guidance in. This will help you to target the right person or organization that can provide you with the support you need.

2. **Seek out mentors:** Reach out to individuals or organizations that specialize in your area of interest. Look for people who have experience and knowledge in your field and who are willing to share their expertise with you.

3. **Join groups:** Join groups or organizations that cater to your interests. This will give you access to a network of professionals who can offer mentorship and guidance.

4. **Attend events:** Attend events and conferences related to your field. This is a great way to meet new people, learn about new trends and developments, and get advice from experts.

5. **Use online resources:** Several online platforms offer mentorship and guidance services. Look for online communities or forums related to your field and participate actively.

6. **Be proactive:** Don't wait for mentorship and guidance to come to you. Be proactive in seeking out opportunities and building relationships with people who can help you achieve your goals.

Mentorship and guidance are important for personal and professional growth. Don't be afraid to ask for help or seek out new opportunities for learning and development.

Chapter 9

ACHIEVING SUCCESS

Achieving success can mean different things to different people, as it is a subjective concept that can vary based on individual goals, values, and aspirations. In general, however, success is often defined as the attainment of a desired outcome or goal that brings a sense of accomplishment, satisfaction, or fulfillment.

Success can be seen as reaching a specific milestone, such as graduating from college, starting a business, getting a promotion, or earning a certain amount of money. However, it can also be viewed as a more ongoing process of personal growth and development, where one continually strives to improve and achieve new goals.

Ultimately, achieving success is a personal journey that requires hard work, dedication, and perseverance. It involves setting goals, developing a plan of action, and putting in the effort required to reach those goals. While success may look different for everyone, it often involves a combination of determination, resilience, and a willingness to learn and grow along the way.

Celebrating your successes and reflecting on your progress

Celebrating your successes and reflecting on your progress are important practices that can help you stay motivated and focused on achieving your goals. Celebrating your successes involves recognizing and acknowledging the milestones you have achieved along the way. It can be something as simple as giving yourself a pat on the back or treating yourself to something you enjoy. Celebrating your successes helps to boost your confidence, reinforces positive behavior, and encourages you to keep moving forward.

Reflecting on your progress involves taking time to evaluate how far you have come and what you have learned along the way. This can help you identify areas where you have improved, as well as areas where you may need to focus more attention. Reflection also allows you to adjust your goals and strategies as needed to continue making progress.

1. **Write it down:** Keep a journal or a list of all your successes, accomplishments, and milestones. Write down the date, the achievement, and how it made you feel. This will help you reflect on your progress and give you a sense of pride and accomplishment.

2. **Treat yourself:** Reward yourself for your accomplishments. This could be as simple as

treating yourself to your favorite meal or indulging in a hobby that you enjoy.

3. **Share your success:** Share your accomplishments with others, such as friends, family, or colleagues. They will likely be happy for you and this will also give you a chance to reflect on your journey and progress.

4. **Reflect on your journey:** Take some time to reflect on how far you have come and what you have learned along the way. This will help you appreciate your successes and also identify areas where you can continue to improve.

5. **Set new goals:** After celebrating your successes and reflecting on your progress, it's time to set new goals. This will help you continue to grow and develop, and give you something to work towards.

Remember to take the time to celebrate your successes and reflect on your progress. It's important to acknowledge your hard work and achievements and also to continue to strive towards new goals.

Giving back and contributing to the success of others

Giving back and contributing to the success of others is a noble and fulfilling endeavor that can bring a sense of purpose and satisfaction to your life. Here are a few ways you can contribute to the success of others:

1. **Volunteer your time:** Volunteering is a great way to give back to your community and help others succeed. You can volunteer at a local non-profit organization or charity, mentor someone who is struggling, or simply offer your time to those in need.

2. **Share your knowledge and expertise:** If you have a particular skill or area of expertise, consider sharing it with others who could benefit from it. This could involve teaching a class or workshop, offering your services as a consultant or coach, or mentoring someone who is just starting in your field.

3. **Support small businesses and entrepreneurs:** Small businesses and entrepreneurs are the backbone of our economy, and supporting them can help contribute to their success. You can do this by buying locally-made products, promoting small businesses on social media, or even investing in a small start-up.

4. **Donate to charities and non-profit organizations:** Charities and non-profit organizations are always in need of financial support to continue their work. Consider donating money or resources to a cause that is important to you, or volunteering your time to help them with their fundraising efforts.

Contributing to the success of others doesn't have to be a grand gesture. Even small acts of kindness and support can make a big difference in someone's life.

CONCLUSIONS

After exploring the principles and strategies behind success, it becomes clear that success is not a product of luck or circumstance, but rather the result of deliberate and consistent effort. A success blueprint must be based on a foundation of hard work, resilience, and a willingness to take risks.

The key to success lies in setting clear goals, creating a detailed plan, and committing to the necessary actions to achieve those goals. Success also requires a growth mindset, where one is constantly learning and adapting to new challenges and opportunities.

Another important aspect of a success blueprint is the ability to cultivate strong relationships and networks. Ultimately, success is not a destination but a journey. It is important to celebrate the small wins and learn from the failures along the way. With dedication, perseverance, and a well-crafted success blueprint, anyone can achieve their goals and reach their full potential.

Reviewing your success blueprint and making adjustments

Reviewing your success blueprint and making adjustments is a crucial step in achieving long-term success. This process involves regularly assessing your goals, strategies, and actions to determine if they are still relevant and effective in helping you reach your desired outcomes.

The first step in reviewing your success blueprint is to revisit your goals and assess whether they are still aligned with your values and aspirations. If your goals have changed, it may be necessary to adjust your strategies and actions accordingly.

Next, evaluate the effectiveness of your current strategies and actions. Are they helping you make progress toward your goals? Are there any areas where you need to improve or adjust your approach? This step requires honesty and self-reflection to identify areas for improvement.

It's also important to seek feedback from others, whether it's from a mentor, coach, or trusted friend. This can help you gain new perspectives and identify blind spots in your thinking or actions. Based on your assessments and feedback, make any necessary adjustments to your success blueprint. This may involve modifying your goals, refining your strategies, or taking different actions to achieve your desired outcomes.

Finally, regularly monitor your progress and make ongoing adjustments as needed. Success is a dynamic process, and staying flexible and adaptable can help you stay on track and achieve your goals over time.

By staying committed to this process, you can increase your chances of achieving long-term success.

Embracing a lifelong journey of growth and success.

Embracing a lifelong journey of growth and success is a mindset that requires commitment, perseverance, and a willingness to learn and adapt.

- **Learn continuously:** Make a habit of learning new things every day. Read books, take online courses, attend workshops or conferences, and seek out mentors or coaches who can help you develop new skills and knowledge.

- **Embrace failure:** Failure is a natural part of the learning process. Rather than being intimidated by setbacks, use them as a chance and opportunity to learn and grow. Analyze your mistakes, identify what you can do differently next time, and keep moving forward.

- **Stay curious:** Keep an open mind and stay curious about the world around you. Ask questions, seek out new experiences, and be willing to take risks and try new things.

- **Cultivate a growth mindset:** A growth mindset is a belief that your abilities and intelligence can be developed through hard work and dedication. Adopt challenges, persist through barriers, and obstacles, and believe in your ability to learn and grow.

- **Surround yourself with positive influences:** Surround yourself with people who inspire and motivate you. Seek out mentors, peers, and colleagues who share your values and goals and who can provide support and guidance along the way.

- **Practice self-care:** Taking care of your physical and mental well-being is necessary for long-term success. Make time for exercise, leisure, and amusements that bring you joy and fulfillment.

By following these tips and committing to a lifelong journey of growth and success, you can achieve your goals and become the best version of yourself.

60-Days SUCCESS CHALLENGE

Here's a 60-day challenge that can help you create a successful blueprint and achieve your goals:

Day 1-10: Define Your Vision

- Write down your long-term goals and vision for success.
- Break down your long-term goals into smaller, achievable goals.
- Identify your strengths and weaknesses.
- Start building your personal and professional network.
- Create a vision board to help you stay focused on your goals.

Day 11-20: Plan Your Success

- Develop a detailed action plan for achieving your goals.
- Set deadlines for each milestone.
- Establish daily and weekly routines to help you stay on track.
- Identify potential obstacles and develop strategies to overcome them.
- Hold yourself accountable by tracking your progress.

Day 21-30: Build Your Skills

- Identify the skills you need to achieve your goals.

- Develop a plan for acquiring those skills.
- Read books, attend workshops or seminars, and seek out mentors to help you develop your skills.
- Practice your skills regularly.
- Stay motivated and focused by tracking your progress and celebrating your achievements.

Day 31-40: Take Action
- Start implementing your action plan.
- Take small, consistent steps toward your goals every day.
- Don't be afraid to take risks and try new things.
- Learn from your mistakes and use them as opportunities to grow.
- Stay flexible and adjust your plan as necessary.

Day 41-50: Build Momentum
- Celebrate your progress and accomplishments.
- Keep pushing yourself to achieve more.
- Share your successes with others to build momentum and motivation.
- Stay focused on your vision and goals.
- Use positive self-talk to stay motivated and confident.

Day 51-60: Stay Committed
- Stay committed to your goals, even when things get tough.
- Don't give up on your dreams.
- Find inspiration and motivation in others who have achieved similar success.

- Stay disciplined and focused on your daily routines and habits.
- Remember why you started and keep pushing forward.

Good luck with your challenge! Remember that success is a journey, not a destination, and that each step you take towards your goals is a success in itself.